D1334695

Published by Top That! Publishing plc
Tide Mill Way, Woodbridge, Suffolk, IP12 1AP, UK
www.topthatpublishing.com
Copyright © 2013 Top That! Publishing plc
All rights reserved
0 2 4 6 8 9 7 5 3 1
Printed and bound in China

Creative Director – Simon Couchman
Editorial Director – Daniel Graham

Illustrated by Daniel Howarth
Written by Peter Shaw

All rights reserved. No part of this publication may be reproduced, stored in a retrieval system, or transmitted in any form or by any means, electronic, mechanical, photocopying, recording or otherwise, without the prior written permission of the publisher. Neither this book nor any part or any of the illustrations, photographs or reproductions contained in it shall be sold or disposed of otherwise than as a complete book, and any unauthorised sale of such part illustration, photograph or reproduction shall be deemed to be a breach of the publisher's copyright.

ISBN 978-1-84956-778-7

A catalogue record for this book is available from the British Library
Printed and bound in China

Little Ronnie and Magic the Horse

Written by Peter Shaw

'For Jessica, my inspiration,
My little ray of sunshine,
You'll never know a love as strong,
As the love you'll get of mine.

From your loving Daddy x'
Peter Shaw

Ronnie was delighted with his new birthday toy,
A white rocking horse that was just right for a boy.
With a long purple tail and a silky mane,
Ronnie decided to give it a name.

'You'll be "Magic" ... "Magic the horse".'
Ronnie never thought Magic would be magic, of course!
He jumped on the stallion, without looking back.
The room started swirling, before it turned black ...

Now Magic was real, and they no longer stood,
In Ronnie's bedroom, but a mysterious wood.

There were flowers and trees, but where was his bed?
And in place of a wardrobe there were rocks instead!

Beyond the trees was a castle in the distance,
Ronnie could scarcely believe its existence.
So off they sped, to meet the Queen and King,
Of the enchanted world they found themselves in.

Soon they arrived and they were met at the gates,
By a guard who was grumpy and a bit overweight.
'You're late,' he said. 'You'd better go in.
You're braver than me, being late for the King!'

They followed his directions to the King's quarters,
And the hustle and bustle of the servants and porters.
'We thought you'd forgotten – at last, you've arrived!'
Cried the beautiful Queen, with tears in her eyes.

'I'm afraid there's a dragon,' the King then sighed.
'His roar can be heard from far and wide.
He's frightening our people and we've had enough.
We need your help, Ronnie,' he said, with a huff.

'I'll see what I can do, but it won't be easy,'
Said Ronnie, sounding brave, but feeling queasy.
'So giddiup, Magic,' and they galloped off with a neigh.
Would Ronnie and his noble steed find their way?

A few hours passed (and gosh they went fast),
When a roar filled the air – they'd found
the dragon at last ...

'Is that him, Magic?' asked Ronnie, with a snigger.
'He doesn't look scary and I thought he'd be bigger!'
He was slimy and scaly, but most strangely of all,
The troublesome dragon was incredibly small!

'We can't fight this dragon; he's done nothing wrong.
We'll go back to the castle, and take him along.
We can't leave him here all on his own,
Perhaps he'll stop roaring if we give him a home.'

So back to the castle and to the King's quarters,
And the hustle and bustle of the servants and porters.
'Allow me to introduce ...' Ronnie said, with a smile,
'The dragon that's caused trouble all this while.'

'Is it true,' laughed the Queen, 'that this little thing,
Has scared all the people and even the King?'

'It's true,' said Ronnie, 'and I've got an idea!
It will stop him from roaring throughout the year.
Why not give him a home, his very own house?
And in return he will be as quiet as a mouse.'

They agreed to the deal, and the dragon was invited,
To live by the castle; he was truly delighted!

Ronnie turned up that evening for his reward,
Riding on Magic, he was greeted with applause.
Ronnie was happy; he felt extremely excited,
As he knelt before the King, ready to be knighted.

'Arise, Sir Ronnie,' and the crowd cheered.
Ronnie looked up ... but they'd all disappeared!

Now Ronnie was back in his bedroom once more,
There was his bed and his old chest of drawers.
'I got off Magic,' Ronnie said with dismay,
'And it made my adventure vanish away.'

And sure enough, Magic stood wooden and lifeless,
But Ronnie knew Magic WAS magic and priceless.

More great picture books from Top That! Publishing

ISBN 978-1-84956-610-0

A fox cub experiences his first summer in this heart-warming storybook.

ISBN 978-1-78244-064-2

A humorous storybook, full of nonsense, by inimitable author, Edward Lear.

ISBN 978-1-84956-245-4

Unique illustrations capture the loving bond between two best friends!

ISBN 978-1-78244-040-6

Follow the little raindrop's adventure and learn all about the water cycle.

ISBN 978-1-78244-074-1

Cammy the colourful Chameleon learns an important lesson in this vibrant tale.

ISBN 978-1-84956-304-8

Milly the meerkat learns a very important lesson in this classic tale.

ISBN 978-1-84956-302-4

Follow the antics of the escaped zoo animals as they cause pandamonium!

ISBN 978-1-78244-059-8

Peter's pebbles come to life in this perfectly crafted tale, full of imagination.

ISBN 978-1-78244-073-4

This tale, full of fun and folly, recalls the Quangle Wangle and his delightful hat.

ISBN 978-1-84956-424-3

A wise owl refuses to bow to peer pressure in this amusing, rhyming tale.

ISBN 978-1-84956-438-0

A fantastical tale about unruly, morning hair and a mischievous fairy.

ISBN 978-1-84956-439-7

The animal food chain is turned upside-down in this funny story with a twist.

Available from all good bookstores or visit www.topthatpublishing.com